Wolverhampton
TROLLEYBUSES
1961-67

Graham Sidwell
Series editor Robert J Harley

MP *Middleton Press*

Cover photographs:

Front cover
Sunbeam W 409, with its second Park Royal body, is on Newhampton Road East, passing Wolverhampton's Municipal Grammar School on the way to Whitmore Reans in August 1965. In the background are the floodlights of Wolverhampton Wanderers' Molineux ground. This was the first major electric tram route, opened on 1 May 1902 to serve the Wolverhampton Art and Industrial Exhibition in West Park, to the right of the trolleybus. Trolleybuses started on 27 January 1930.

Back Cover
Commercial Road Power Station provides the backdrop as Sunbeam W 416 crosses the bridge over the Birmingham Canal Navigations on a journey to Darlaston on the last day of trolleybuses on the route, 8 August 1965. The power station was opened by Lord Kelvin in 1895, long before electric trams came to Bilston Road in 1902. Electric trams came back in 1999, as this is the route followed by Midland Metro before it turns onto the formation of the former railway line to Birmingham Snow Hill at Monmore Green.

Published September 2006

ISBN 1 904474 85 3

© *Middleton Press, 2006*

Design Deborah Esher

Published by
    Middleton Press
    Easebourne Lane
    Midhurst, West Sussex
    GU29 9AZ
Tel: 01730 813169
Fax: 01730 812601
Email: info@middletonpress.co.uk
www.middletonpress.co.uk

Printed & bound by Biddles Ltd, Kings Lynn

CONTENTS

INTRODUCTION AND ACKNOWLEDGEMENTS

The principal source for any history of Wolverhampton's trolleybuses is a document written by the transport department's long-serving chief clerk, Osmond Wildsmith. This was first serialised in the Express & Star in 1961 and was subsequently edited and expanded by Stanley Webb and Paul Addenbrooke into the two-volume semi-official history Wolverhampton Corporation Transport. The present author contributed to both volumes and has reproduced some material he originally created for it, principally the Dates of Operation table and the depot diagrams.

Andy Simpson and Roy Clark wrote a series detailing the trolleybus system in the Black Country Museum Transport Group Newsletter. John Hughes and David Harvey collaborated to produce the three-volume Wolverhampton by tram, bus and trolleybus. The present author has written about the momentous events of 1963 (the first major abandonments in Wolverhampton and the last Black Country route extension in Walsall) in Classic Bus. However, the author's notes, log books and memories form the largest source for the captions and text.

In creating the maps afresh, the author acknowledges the work of E. K. (Keith) Stretch, whose 1961 diagram was the first to record the system.

The photographs of the Bennett Clark Studio, Ray Wilson (courtesy of The Omnibus Society), Robin Hannay, Deryk Vernon, Stanley Webb, S.N.J. White and Cliff Brown have all appeared in print at various times, as have some of the author's own, and it is difficult to avoid repetition. In this case I have used my own archive to show the decline of the trolleybuses and some of the more unusual features of the system, and used largely unpublished material. Where the work is not my own I have acknowledged the source in the caption.

I have mercilessly and gratefully picked John Hughes' brains and record books to fill the (I am surprised to find minor though important) gaps in my records.

The author is presently the honorary editor of Tramfare, the bi-monthly journal of the Tramway and Light Railway Society.

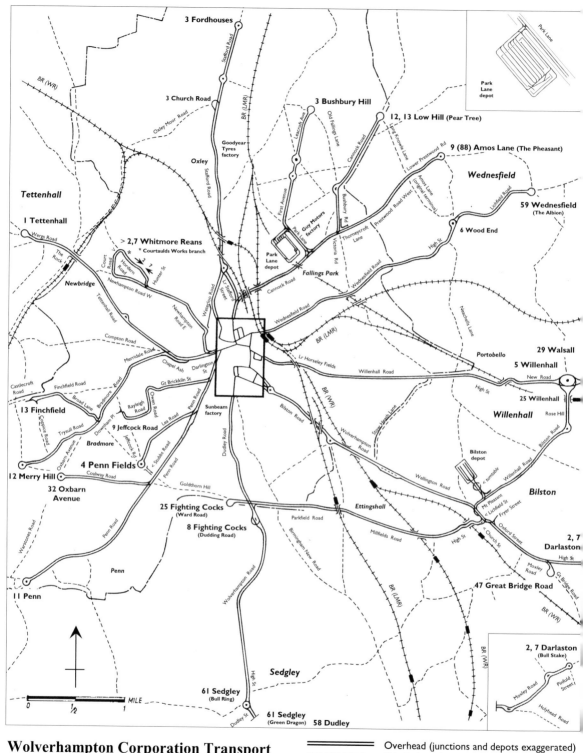

Wolverhampton Corporation Transport
Trolleybus network at 31 December 1960
© 2006 L G Sidwell. Map drawn by Clive Beech.

───────	Overhead (junctions and depots exaggerated)
- - - - - -	Principal roads
++++++++	Railways
- · - · - · -	County Borough boundary

Key map labels:

3 Fordhouses

Park Lane depot

3 Church Road

BR (WR)

BR (LMR)

Oxley Moor Road

Stafford Road

Goodyear Tyres factory

Oxley

Stafford Road

3 Bushbury Hill

Leacroft Ave

Old Fallings Lane

Cannock Road

12, 13 Low Hill (Pear Tree)

Ling Knowle Lane

9 (88) Amos Lane (The Pheasant)

Lower Prestwood Rd

Wednesfield

Lichfield Road

59 Wednesfield (The Albion)

Tettenhall

1 Tettenhall

Wergs Road

The Rock

> 2, 7 Whitmore Reans
* Courtaulds Works branch

Court Road

Hordern Road

Hunter St

First Avenue

Park Lane

Guy Motors factory

Park Lane depot

Bushbury Rd

Amos Lane (original terminal)

Prestwood Road West

Thorneycroft Lane

Victoria Rd

High St

6 Wood End

Newbridge

Tettenhall Road

Newhampton Road W

Newhampton Road E

Cannock Road

Fallings Park

Wednesfield Road

Wednesfield Road

Neachells Lane

Compton Road

Merridale Road

Chapel Ash

Darlington St

Wednesfield Road

Lr Horseley Fields

BR (LMR)

Portobello

29 Walsall

5 Willenhall

Castlecroft Road

Finchfield Road

Bradmore Road

Gt Brickkiln St

Willenhall Road

New Road

Coppice Road

Trysull Road

Broad Lane

Rayleigh Road

Owen Road

Penn Road

Lea Road

Penn Road

Sunbeam factory

Bilston Road

BR (WR)

Wolverhampton Road

Stow Heath Lane

High St

25 Willenhall

Willenhall

Rose Hill

Bilston Road

13 Finchfield

9 Jeffcock Road

Jeffcock Rd

Bradmore

Squabb Road

Dudley Road

Bilston depot

< turntable

4 Penn Fields

12 Merry Hill

Coalway Road

Penn Road

Goldthorn Hill

Wellington Road

Willenhall Road

Mt Pleasant

Bilston

32 Oxbarn Avenue

25 Fighting Cocks (Ward Road)

8 Fighting Cocks (Dudding Road)

Parkfield Road

Ettingshall

Millfields Road

High St

< Lichfield St

< Fryer Street

Oxford Street

< Church St

2, 7 Darlaston

High St

Penn Road

Birmingham New Road

Wolverhampton Road

Moxley Road

Gt Bridge Road

Warstones Road

47 Great Bridge Road

BR (WR)

11 Penn

Penn

BR (LMR)

Sedgley

High St

61 Sedgley (Bull Ring)

Dudley St

61 Sedgley (Green Dragon)

58 Dudley

2, 7 Darlaston (Bull Stake)

Moxley Road

Pinfold Street

Holyhead Road

MILE

0   ½   1

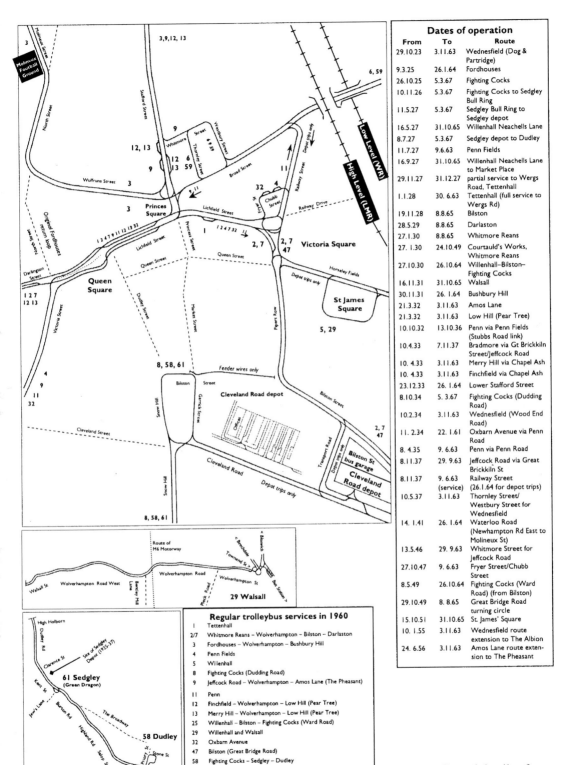

Dates of operation

From	To	Route
29.10.23	3.11.63	Wednesfield (Dog & Partridge)
9.3.25	26.1.64	Fordhouses
26.10.25	5.3.67	Fighting Cocks
10.11.26	5.3.67	Fighting Cocks to Sedgley Bull Ring
11.5.27	5.3.67	Sedgley Bull Ring to Sedgley depot
16.5.27	31.10.65	Willenhall Neachells Lane
8.7.27	5.3.67	Sedgley depot to Dudley
11.7.27	9.6.63	Penn Fields
16.9.27	31.10.65	Willenhall Neachells Lane to Market Place
29.11.27	31.12.27	partial service to Wergs Road, Tettenhall
1.1.28	30.6.63	Tettenhall (full service to Wergs Rd)
19.11.28	8.8.65	Bilston
28.5.29	8.8.65	Darlaston
27.1.30	8.8.65	Whitmore Reans
27.1.30	24.10.49	Courtauld's Works, Whitmore Reans
27.10.30	26.10.64	Willenhall–Bilston–Fighting Cocks
16.11.31	31.10.65	Walsall
30.11.31	26.1.64	Bushbury Hill
21.3.32	3.11.63	Amos Lane
21.3.32	3.11.63	Low Hill (Pear Tree)
10.10.32	13.10.36	Penn via Penn Fields (Stubbs Road link)
10.4.33	7.11.37	Bradmore via Gt Brickkiln Street/Jeffcock Road
10.4.33	3.11.63	Merry Hill via Chapel Ash
10.4.33	3.11.63	Finchfield via Chapel Ash
23.12.33	26.1.64	Lower Stafford Street
8.10.34	5.3.67	Fighting Cocks (Dudding Road)
10.2.34	3.11.63	Wednesfield (Wood End Road)
11.2.34	22.1.61	Oxbarn Avenue via Penn Road
8.4.35	9.6.63	Penn via Penn Road
8.11.37	29.9.63	Jeffcock Road via Great Brickkiln St
8.11.37	9.6.63 (service) (26.1.64 for depot trips)	Railway Street
10.5.37	3.11.63	Thornley Street/Westbury Street for Wednesfield
14.1.41	26.1.64	Waterloo Road (Newhampton Rd East to Molineux St)
13.5.46	29.9.63	Whitmore Street for Jeffcock Road
27.10.47	9.6.63	Fryer Street/Chubb Street
8.5.49	26.10.64	Fighting Cocks (Ward Road) (from Bilston)
29.10.49	8.8.65	Great Bridge Road turning circle
15.10.51	31.10.65	St. James' Square
10.1.55	3.11.63	Wednesfield route extension to The Albion
24.6.56	3.11.63	Amos Lane route extension to The Pheasant

Regular trolleybus services in 1960

1	Tettenhall
2/7	Whitmore Reans – Wolverhampton – Bilston – Darlaston
3	Fordhouses – Wolverhampton – Bushbury Hill
4	Penn Fields
5	Willenhall
8	Fighting Cocks (Dudding Road)
9	Jeffcock Road – Wolverhampton – Amos Lane (The Pheasant)
11	Penn
12	Finchfield – Wolverhampton – Low Hill (Pear Tree)
13	Merry Hill – Wolverhampton – Low Hill (Pear Tree)
25	Willenhall – Bilston – Fighting Cocks (Ward Road)
29	Willenhall and Walsall
32	Oxbarn Avenue
47	Bilston (Great Bridge Road)
58	Fighting Cocks – Sedgley – Dudley
59	Wednesfield (The Albion) (6 Wood End short working)
61	Fighting Cocks – Sedgley (Bull Ring or Green Dragon)

Central details of map shown on left page

GEOGRAPHICAL SETTING

Wolverhampton derives its name from its location (Heantun or Hamptun or High Town), whose principal church of St Peter is 650ft above sea level, and its main benefactress, the Lady Wulfrun, hence Wulfrun's Hamptun. Its earliest origins trace to 985, when King Ethelred II (The Unready) gave the lands to his sister Lady Wulfrun, (or Wulfruna, opinions vary). Granted a market charter in 1258, the town became a major centre of the wool trade, celebrated to this day in street names like Farmers Fold.

The Industrial Revolution, with roots nearby in Coalbrookdale, and the subsequent exploitation of the rich mineral resources of the Black Country to the south, could have passed Wolverhampton by. Purists define the Black Country by the limits of the six yard coal seam and Wolverhampton is not above it and therefore not in it. But its entrepreneurs took up metalworking trades, including lockmaking, and the town prospered on them and on commerce, helped by the coming of the canals in 1772 and the railways in 1838. Joseph Armstrong made Wolverhampton the Northern Headquarters of the Great Western Railway and the loco works was an important source of employment until the 1960s.

Cycle manufacturing in the late Victorian period naturally graduated into motorcycles and cars; Clyno and Star were early attempts to set up in car making. John Marston's japanning factory turned "Sunbeam" into a household word for all three modes, and the factory and surrounding area of the town became "Sunbeamland". One of his employees, the works manager, Sydney Guy, set himself up in commercial motor manufacturing in 1914. Sunbeam made trolleybuses in later years and all but the first 32 of Wolverhampton's trolleybus fleet came from these two companies.

HISTORICAL BACKGROUND

Horse trams of the Wolverhampton Tramways Co began on 1 May 1878, while steam trams operated to Dudley from 1886 after a period of horse operation. The tramways were municipalised in 1900 and, from 1902, rebuilt from 4ft 8½in / 1435mm to 3ft 6in / 1067mm and electrified using the Lorain Surface Contact System, until it was replaced by overhead wires in 1921.

General manager Charles Owen Silvers recommended converting worn out tram routes to trolleybuses. He may have been inspired by the conversion on 27 November 1922 of Birmingham's single-track Nechells route to trolleybuses. The council went to see it, gave approval in March 1923 and things moved quickly. The Wednesfield route closed as a tramway on 23 July 1923. The trolleybus service opened to the public on 29 October 1923. Meanwhile Ipswich had also converted its first tram route to trolleybuses, beating Wolverhampton by seven weeks.

Silvers had evidently been dissatisfied with the tram-like vehicles of the early trolleybus systems, and persuaded petrol-electric bus manufacturer Tilling-Stevens (the corporation already had a few) to remove the petrol engines from six of its TS6 chassis and convert them to straight electric. He also seems to have persuaded British Thompson-Houston to develop a new control system.

Instead of bulky hand-operated tram-style controllers, BTH developed a foot pedal drum type, precursor of all subsequent trolleybus controllers, with remotely-operated contactors switching the controlling resistances. The motor set-up emulated that of a tram, with two armatures on the same shaft and the controller switching them from series to parallel as it notched up. The advent of compound winding did away with the need for that in due course. So Wolverhampton's Dodson-bodied trolleybuses looked and drove like the conventional solid-tyred buses of the day.

The tram route to Bushbury was closed for conversion on 19 August 1924. The trolleybuses went right to the town boundary at the Vine Inn, Fordhouses, starting on 9 March 1925. Single deckers again, as both routes were troubled by low railway bridges, and the fleet of the Tilling Stevens vehicles eventually reached 32.

The long route through Fighting Cocks and Sedgley opened on 16 October 1925 and through to Dudley from 8 July 1927, with single deckers. Local manufacturer Guy Motors came up with the first three-axle, pneumatic tyred, regenerative braked, open-staircase, covered top double deck trolleybus in 1927, and it was quickly followed by more, though with closed staircases. No 33 was eventually preserved, only to be scrapped for the war effort in the 1940s.

The tram routes were all closed by 1928 (the last tram ran to Bilston on 26 August 1928) and converted by October 1930. The corporation had even taken over some company tram routes over the town boundary, with a view to conversion. At the end of 1930 Wolverhampton's 70-strong fleet made it the largest trolleybus operator in the country.

By the 1930s the town was expanding and needed public transport to serve new housing estates. It came usually in the form of a petrol-engined motor bus, but the route north to Bushbury Hill was electrified from

30 November 1931, followed in March 1932 by the other two Cannock Road routes to Amos Lane and Low Hill. Older suburbs to the west quickly followed: Bradmore, Finchfield and Merry Hill in April 1933, and finally Oxbarn Avenue in February 1934. After that came only diversionary wiring and three short post-war extensions, the last to The Pheasant on the Amos Lane route on 24 June 1956.

Transport policy had been kept under review since the first conversion. In January 1939 the newly-developed oil (diesel) engine was felt by the general manager to have a "slight advantage" over electric traction. The corporation decided to stick with trolleybuses for the next 10 years, renewing the fleet completely during and after the war. The war prolonged the lives of many vehicles (and brought Bournemouth trolleybuses and their crews to work in the town) and the next full review seems to have been in January 1957, just after the Suez Crisis emphasised the importance of home-produced fuels.

That review, by Silvers's successor Robert Hopewell Addlesee who took over in 1949, found an ageing fleet whose future would be decided "on its merits". Orders for 38 new bodies followed. The trolleybus fleet at the end of 1960 totalled 153 vehicles, with some156 motorbuses.

In March 1961 Addlesee pointed out that 91 of the 153 trolleybuses would need replacing within four years. The lead time for new vehicles would be all of that, and cost £1,200 per vehicle more than the equivalent diesel. The national trend was to get rid of trolleybuses. The route-bound nature of the trolleybus militated against operational flexibility in a town proposing to alter its road network with an inner ring road (completed in the 1980s) and one-way streets (never successfully adopted). In May 1961 the council decided to operate the trolleybus system "to the end of its useful life". By then the first route had already been abandoned.

The 32 route along Coalway Road to Oxbarn Avenue was replaced without anyone realising its disappearance. From 23 January 1961 the corporation embarked on the construction of the borough's first pedestrian subway in the town centre and had to divert traffic away from the site, close some roads and make others one way only. This meant that trolleybuses on the Penn Road routes, 4, 9, 11 and 32, had to be temporarily replaced with motorbuses, and 20 old Daimlers were hired from Birmingham City Transport for the duration. When the trolleybuses came back on 22 May 1961, there was no route 32. The last trolleybus on 22 January is believed to have been Guy BT 652. The first casualties after the council formalised the abandonment of the trolleybus system were the remaining Penn Road services 4 (Penn Fields, last trolleybus 498) and 11 (Penn, 606), which were withdrawn on Sunday 9 June 1963.

Next came Tettenhall (622), on 30 June, followed by the last route down Worcester Street to Jeffcock Road on 29 September 1963. The last trolleybus was 423, while 475, the first to use the new extension in 1956, worked the last cross-town journey from Jeffcock Road. The route was then split and the Amos Lane section took the route number 88 and turned in Princes Square, until 3 November 1963 when there was a wholesale clearout.

The 88 (last trolleybus 451), together with the 12 (441) and 13 (444) Cannock Road services to Low Hill and the cross-town Bradmore services to Merry Hill (13, 616) and Finchfield (12, 444), and the pioneering route to Wednesfield (59, 446) all ran their last. That left only the Fordhouses and Bushbury Hill (3) trolleybuses running from Park Lane depot to await the next delivery of replacement motor buses.

Meanwhile, roadworks to construct a dual carriageway on Stafford Road north of Oxley Moor Road meant that the overhead line department had to erect new wires. The trolleybuses used the new section of road for just a fortnight until they were abandoned on 26 January 1964. 448 was the last from Fordhouses, 439 the last from Bushbury Hill.

Ironically, while road transport was being dieselised, British Railways was busy electrifying the West Coast Main Line through Wolverhampton, including the Grand Junction line through Willenhall. Many bridges had to be raised and one in Willenhall forced the closure of the 25 trolleybus to Bilston and Fighting Cocks on 25 October 1964, despite an offer from BR to fund a temporary turning point. 408 was the last from Willenhall, 440 the last from Fighting Cocks.

The last cross-town routes from Whitmore Reans to Bilston and Darlaston (2/7 and 47) closed on 8 August 1965. 422 was the last on route 2 from Whitmore Reans, 432 the last route 7; 446 was the last to Darlaston and 409 the last to turn at Great Bridge Road (47). Preservation candidate 433 was the last to leave Bilston Depot for service. The Walsall route was a victim of motorway construction and closed on 31 October 1965. The last bus on route 5 to Willenhall was 432; on the 29 to Walsall, the last Wolverhampton bus was 434, the last Walsall vehicle 353, ex-Ipswich. 446 ran a special late tour for the NTA after the official last vehicles.

The final routes (8, 58 and 61) along Dudley Road soldiered on for another 18 months, served by the remaining 28 vehicles, running their last on Sunday 5 March 1967, without special ceremony. 446 (at the time a candidate for preservation) ran the last trip from Dudley, while 451 is believed to have been the last to take power from Wolverhampton wires as it was removed from Cleveland Road Depot.

Post-war trolleybus fleet

Fleet No	Chassis	Date	Body
402-417	Sunbeam W	1944-45	Park Royal H28/26R
418	Sunbeam W	1945	Roe H32/28R
419-433	Sunbeam W	1946	Roe H32/28R
434-455	Sunbeam W	1947-48	Roe H32/28R
456-481	Sunbeam F4	1948	Park Royal H28/26R
482-499	Guy BT	1949	Park Royal H28/26R
600-607	Guy BT	1949	Park Royal H28/26R
608-630	Sunbeam F4	1949-50	Park Royal H28/26R
631-654	Guy BT	1949-50	Park Royal H28/26R

402-407/409-417/419-433 originally had PRV H30/26R Utility bodies, rebodied PRV (Park Royal) H28/26R in 1952

408 originally had Weymann H30/26R Utility body, rebodied PRV H28/26R in 1952

418 carried its original PRV Utility H30/26R body until rebodied Roe H32/28R in 1958

419-454 originally PRV H30/26R, rebodied Roe H32/28R 1960-62

456 onwards were 8ft wide.

By October 1962 the fleet (153 strong in 1960) was 10 fewer, through scrappings following accidents.

PENN ROAD

1.	Oxbarn Avenue and Penn Fields routes had their town centre termini relocated in 1947 to Chubb Street, a side street between Victoria Square and Railway Street. Alf Yates took this picture of Guy BT 651 at the 32 route terminus not many years afterwards, as the vehicle is still in its early 1950s livery and still has its Guy badge, many of which disappeared in subsequent repaints.

SERVICE 32			WOLVERHAMPTON—OXBARN AVENUE (via Penn Road and Coalway Road)								TROLLEY BUS SERVICE	
MONDAY TO FRIDAY												
WOLVERHAMPTON	Chubb Street	dep.	AM 6 30	AM 6 45	AM 7 0	every 8 minutes	AM 8 44	AM 8 58	every 20 minutes	PM 1238	PM 1 0	every 12 minutes
WOLVERHAMPTON	Oxbarn Avenue	arr.	6 44	6 59	7 14		8 58	9 12		1252	1 14	
WOLVERHAMPTON	Oxbarn Avenue	dep.	AM 6 45	AM 7 0	AM 7 16	every 8 minutes	AM 8 52	AM 9 5	9 22	every 20 minutes	PM 1 2	PM 1 18 ....
WOLVERHAMPTON	Chubb Street	arr.	6 59	7 14	7 30		9 6	9 19	9 36		1 16	1 32 ....
WOLVERHAMPTON	Chubb Street	dep.	PM 4 0		every 8 minutes		PM 6 16	PM 6 25	PM 6 38	every 20 minutes	1038	PM 11 0 ....
WOLVERHAMPTON	Oxbarn Avenue	arr.	4 14				6 30	6 42	6 52		1052	1114 ....
WOLVERHAMPTON	Oxbarn Avenue	dep.	every 12 minutes			PM 4 6	PM 4 16	every 8 minutes	PM 6 32	PM 6 44	PM 7 2	every 20 minutes	PM 11 2	1116
WOLVERHAMPTON	Chubb Street	arr.				4 20	4 30		6 46	6 58	7 16		1116	1130
SATURDAY												
WOLVERHAMPTON	Chubb Street	dep.	AM 6 30	AM 6 45	AM 7 0	every 12 minutes	PM 6 0	PM 6 18	every 20 minutes	PM 1038	PM 11 0 ....
WOLVERHAMPTON	Oxbarn Avenue	arr.	6 44	6 59	7 14		6 14	6 32		1052	1114 ....
WOLVERHAMPTON	Oxbarn Avenue	dep.	AM 6 45	AM 7 0	AM 7 18	every 12 minutes	PM 6 6	PM 6 22	every 20 minutes	PM 11 2	PM 1116 ....
WOLVERHAMPTON	Chubb Street	arr.	6 59	7 14	7 32		6 20	6 36		1116	1130 ....
SUNDAY												
WOLVERHAMPTON	Chubb Street	dep.	PM 1 38	PM 2 18	every 20 minutes	PM 1038	PM 11 0 ....
WOLVERHAMPTON	Oxbarn Avenue	arr.	1 52	2 32		1052	1114 ....
WOLVERHAMPTON	Oxbarn Avenue	dep.	PM 2 2	PM 2 42	every 20 minutes	PM 11 2	PM 1116 ....
WOLVERHAMPTON	Chubb Street	arr.	2 16	2 58		1116	1130 ....

←——— 2. Penn trolleybuses ran up Broad Street, the original Wolverhampton trolleybus route, from their terminus in Railway Street. Here was the first request stop and anxious passengers watch the result of conductor forgetfulness, for the frog where Sunbeam F4 619 has dewired is set for the Thornley Street terminus used by the Wednesfield trolleybuses and should have been pulled to allow 619 to progress unhindered.

←——— 3. After Broad Street, Penn Road trolleybuses turned at Princes Square into Lichfield Street, where the wires divided to sort Victoria Street (Penn Road) traffic from Darlington Street, the two routes dividing at the bottom of Queen Square. No stops for Penn Road trolleybuses in Lichfield Street; the wires crossed over at the top of Queen Square and Penn Road routes loaded at this three-way stop, opposite the equestrian statue of Prince Albert, unveiled by Queen Victoria in 1866, her first public appearance outside London since his death in 1861. The stop flags indicated Penn Fields (4) and Penn (11). The empty arm was used by route 32 (Oxbarn Avenue) until May 1961. Passengers board Sunbeam F4 610 for the journey to Penn Fields one Saturday in April 1963.

4. At the top of Worcester Street the route for Jeffcock Road branched off down Great Brickkiln Street (pronounced "brikk-lin") round the long-established Studio Banerjee photographic studio. Sunbeam F4 457, one of the fleet's more battered specimens, inbound from Penn Fields in June 1963.

5.   St Paul's Church would not last much longer than the trolleybuses after the end of the Penn Road services. Guy BT 643 inbound from Penn Fields has passed a traction pole with a coil of span wire, ready to allow the demolition of the overhead behind the photographer to begin construction of the second phase of Wolverhampton's ring road, and a large traffic island now occupies this site. This was also Sunbeamland, site of John Marston's Sunbeam cycle and motor works, where much of the Wolverhampton trolleybus fleet was built.

6.   The Midland Counties Dairy was built at the junction of Penn Road and Lea Road in 1931 and many of its bottling operations were visible to passengers passing on Penn Road (left) and Lea Road (right) services. Guy BT 495 is inbound from Penn Fields in June 1963.

7. Lea Road's terraced housing saw Wolverhampton's first motor bus route (1905-1909), its last tram route to open (1909-1927), and a trolleybus service to Penn Fields and to Penn before the direct Penn route was built along Penn Road. Guy BT 496 inbound from Penn Fields, passes the feeder at Owen Road in April 1963.

8. Guy BT 641 ————→ 9. After the abandonment of Coalway Road, the next wires is on the parallel Penn to come down were those in Stubbs Road, which linked the Lea Road Road, outside the Royal terminus of the Penn Fields route with Penn Road, and which last Wolverhampton School saw regular service in 1935. Undeterred, the Nottingham Trolleybus (still colloquially known Group scheduled the link as part of a tour in March 1963 and the as the Royal Orphanage) accompanying inspector removes the poles from the Penn Road wires on its way to Penn in before Sunbeam W 439, fresh from the paint shop, is pushed around June 1963. the corner and down the hill.

————→ 10. Penn Fields terminus has changed very little in the years between the end of the trams and the present day. By the 1960s the trees had grown, but the shops seemed almost unaltered, indeed Express Valeting still traded. Ray Wilson photographed Guy 64 of 1930 some time in the mid-1930s.

11.   Pictures of the Oxbarn Avenue route are rare, as it was such a backwater, but fortunately an unidentified photographer caught one of the 8ft wide Guy trolleybuses turning at the peanut-shaped island at the junction of Coalway Road and Oxbarn Avenue, one winter lunchtime in the late 1950s or perhaps 1960. The corporation had powers to continue the route the short distance along Coalway Road to the left to link up with the Merry Hill service. It also had powers to electrify the 35 bus route along Oxbarn Avenue and Warstones Road, behind the photographer.

12.   Penn terminus was one of the turning loops on the system where passengers were officially allowed to remain on the vehicle, thanks to the wide and even then relatively dangerous A449 trunk road that they would otherwise have to cross, from the set down point behind the photographer, to get to the shops and the majority of the houses at Springhill. Guy BT 643 waits its next turn in May 1963.

BRADMORE:
JEFFCOCK ROAD, FINCHFIELD, MERRY HILL

13.   The Bradmore routes served inter-war and post-war housing on the western edge of Wolverhampton and first ran as trolleybus routes in 1933. Initially trolleybuses ran via Jeffcock Road and via Chapel Ash, but the Jeffcock Road section was soon cut back. Route 9 for Jeffcock Road was diverted into Whitmore Street on its cross-town travels in 1946 and Sunbeam W 437 pauses before heading west, just a few days before the route was abandoned in September 1963.

14.　Turning out of Westbury Street into Broad Street is Sunbeam W 407, with its second Park Royal body replacing its utility original.

⟶ 15. Sunbeam W 447 turns into Queen Square on a wintry December 1962 day on the way to Merry Hill. It is on the left-hand set of wires in this extended junction and can overtake Penn Road trolleybuses if necessary.

⟶ 16.　Sunbeam F4 468 at another pre-sorting junction outside the former Wolverhampton Tramways Company horse tram depot at the bottom of Darlington Street. In horse days they attached a trace horse here for the long pull to Queen Square. The trolleybus has taken the left-hand wires to turn for Merridale Road at the end of Chapel Ash.

17.   Sunbeam W 403 pulls up the steepish hill of Rayleigh Road on 26 September 1963, heading for the route 9 terminus at Jeffcock Road after its cross-town journey from Amos Lane. The route has trolleybuses for only a few more days.

→ 18. Downham Place is a conventional reversing triangle, a quiet road off Jeffcock Road where in April 1962 Sunbeam W 440 is turning to return to the layover point in Rayleigh Road behind the photographer. The broken hanger is a typical failure of the Wiseman equipment Wolverhampton used, and would be speedily replaced. The wires originally continued down Jeffcock Road to the right and link up with the Bradmore routes but the route was shortened in 1937.

→ 19.   Sunbeam F4 465 is heading out of the valley of the Graisley Brook on Merridale Road towards Bradmore and Finchfield in November 1962. It will soon pass the end of Jeffcock Road, where for a few years in the 1930s, there was a junction for an alternative service to Bradmore.

20.	Bradmore Junction is where the Bradmore routes split for Finchfield and Merry Hill. A gleaming Sunbeam W 403 is heading for Merry Hill in November 1962 on its cross-town trip from Low Hill. In early days there was a turning triangle here for the service to Bradmore via Jeffcock Road.

————▶ 21. Sunbeam W 424 has passed Bradmore Junction at the top of the hill and is heading for Merry Hill, past the Gunmaker's Arms, a typical inter-war public house. The pub is at the junction of Oxbarn Avenue, which could also have been a trolleybus route if the corporation had exercised its powers.

————▶ 22. Broad Lane looked almost rural, flanked by the field surrounding Bantock House, former residence of industrialist Albert Bantock and long since owned by Wolverhampton Council and put to various purposes, including a museum. Sunbeam W 419 is heading for Finchfield in October 1963.

23.   The sylvan scene is at Finchfield as Sunbeam W 419 waits its next turn across town to Low Hill (Pear Tree) after turning on the unusual reverser off Castlecroft Road. Trolleybuses pulled into Coppice Road nose first, then reversed towards the photographer, before running in front of the New Inn. The feeder pillar is for street lighting, and the photographer's trusty bicycle is also in view.

24.   Merry Hill on the western edge of Wolverhampton is the name of the district as well as the pub at the terminus of route 13, where Sunbeam W 454 is standing at the departure point. The turning circle is the large roundabout behind the trolleybus, a junction where the Oxbarn Avenue route 32 could have linked up if the corporation had exercised its powers. On 22 September 1963, Walsall Sunbeam F4A trolleybus 869 came here as part of a tour that took in the furthest points of the Black Country trolleybus system.

TETTENHALL

25.   The taxi rank in the middle of Victoria Square was until after World War II the town centre layover point for many routes, including the number 1 to Tettenhall. The trams had stood waiting nearby. But by November 1961 when the author took his first recorded trolleybus photograph, the terminal point had long since been moved, so the crew of Sunbeam W 409 must have been on a break. The vehicle is painted in a short-lived reversed livery that was not popular.

26. Sunbeam F4 613 loads at its siding loop outside the GPO in Lichfield Street for another trip to Tettenhall.

27. The double wiring that was installed in the late 1950s to separate Bradmore and Tettenhall services started in Darlington Street outside the former Wolverhampton Tramways Company horse tram depot visible above the Morris Minor. In the last month of operations on 1 June 1963, Guy BT 498 turns on to Chapel Ash, with its large hoarding by one of the town's major employers. Behind, up Salop Street, is the new Retail Market, where the construction of a subway forced the substitution of Penn Road trolleybuses for five months in early 1961.

28. The Halfway House is an inn halfway between London and Holyhead, 130 miles in either direction and this is the A41, the main road to North Wales. Sunbeam W 435 negotiates the traffic island on the way to Tettenhall in November 1962.

29.   On a sunny May day in 1963, Sunbeam W 428 pulls away from the stop at Newbridge. The bridge, dating from 1939, crosses over the Staffordshire and Worcestershire canal, and is just beyond where horse trams terminated. This was the only trolleybus to carry the advertisement for a pet shop in Queen Street and will shortly cross from Wolverhampton into Tettenhall.

30.   Thomas Telford is responsible for The Rock, a cutting through the sandstone ridge as part of his works to improve the Holyhead coach road in the late 18th Century. Sunbeam F4 622 descends The Rock from Upper Green on 26 June 1963, the last day of Tettenhall trolleybuses.

31. This was the view travellers from Shropshire would see as they entered the outskirts of the Black Country conurbation. Tettenhall, however, as a separate urban district, never thought of itself as part of the Black Country. This was where the better off tended to live. In April 1962 Sunbeam F4 481, numerically the last of the 1948 batch of 8ft wide vehicles, waits at the terminus alongside the Swiss Chalet, a refugee from the 1902 Wolverhampton Art and Industrial Exhibition in West Park, installed in 1903 to serve waiting tram passengers.

WHITMORE REANS

32.   The Whitmore Reans route had two identities, depending on which way the trolleybus went to get to the terminus in Court Road. Sunbeam W 410, standing, in April 1964, on the right outside the Victoria Hotel in Victoria Square, would travel to Court Road along Newhampton Road West, while Sunbeam F4 465 on the other side of the square, has come back that way, as route 7.

⟶ 33.   Princes Square had one of the first sets of automatic traffic lights in the country. Because of the turns involved, trolleybuses and other traffic always turned right with the island on the nearside, hence the "Turning Right Keep Right" signs. Sunbeam W 406 crosses Princes Square for Victoria Square and onward to Darlaston in December 1963.

⟶ 34. Sunbeam W 408 has taken the inside wires at the pre-sort junction at the top of Darlington Street to turn onto Waterloo Road in front of the Gas Office showroom on its journey to Court Road via Newhampton Road West in June 1963.

35. Sunbeam W 417 eases out of Newhampton Road East onto Waterloo Road near the Molineux football ground, home of Wolverhampton Wanderers, in June 1963. The 1941 connection along Waterloo Road is just visible; the section was never connected to the network and consequently never used. The distant Courtaulds factory chimney is near the Whitmore Reans terminus.

→ 36. Leicester Square, complete with its cast iron Vespasian urinal, was the original 1902 terminus of the Whitmore Reans trams. The trolleybuses served the inhabitants better, reaching along Newhampton Road West almost to Tettenhall Road near Newbridge, before turning onto Court Road to return via Hordern Road and Hunter Street. Sunbeam W 406 has rejoined the common section on its way to Wolverhampton and Darlaston in January 1964.

→ 37. Hunter Street was eventually the normal terminus for Whitmore Reans trams, but the trolleybuses needed a turning loop, provided by Hunter Street itself, Hordern Road and Court Road. Sunbeam F4 625 returns to Newhampton Road West after its trip round the loop as service 2, in April 1964. Route 7 ran in the other direction.

38.   Sunbeam F4 479 is on route 7 in Hordern Road near Wullon Street, at the Three Crowns in May 1964. Just round the bend was the entrance to Courtaulds artificial fibres factory, site of a trolleybus branch until 1949.

39.   The smoking chimney was the visible evidence of the large Courtaulds factory that dominated the area from the 1920s until the early 1970s. Sunbeam F4 624 is standing at the route 2 layover point in Court Road in April 1962. The number 7 went in the other direction, turning from Hordern Road around the Golden Eagle public house.

FORDHOUSES

40.　　Sunbeam Ws 454 (left for Bushbury Hill) and 451 for Fordhouses stand each side of the wide Wulfruna Street on the last day of operation, 26 January 1964. The imposing buildings of the Wolverhampton and South Staffordshire College of Technology to the left were opened in 1933 and now form the main campus of Wolverhampton University.

Xm 56575
WOLVERHAMPTON C. B.
3d | Issued Subject to Bye-Laws and Regulations
ADULT | CHILD
01
HUNT. | NOTTM.

41. Fordhouses trolleybuses originally continued to the right along North Street, Queen Square and Lichfield Street to turn into Wulfruna Street. When the Fordhouses route was linked in 1933 to the Wednesfield route, the wiring was doubled in Wulfruna Street and North Street was removed. In November 1963 Sunbeam W 442 turns out of Wulfruna Street to North Street, at the imposing Chequer Ball public house. The collegiate church of St Peter, its foundation dating to Saxon times, stands at the highest point of the town.

→ 42. Sunbeam W 436 has climbed Molineux Street for the town centre and Bushbury Hill while 441 descends for Fordhouses past the Wolverhampton Wanderers football ground in November 1963. The street was for many years closed on Saturday afternoons to accommodate thousands of football fans going to watch in the team's heyday. The ground's early floodlight towers helped the club stage some of the pioneering 1960s international friendlies with teams from the Soviet Bloc.

→ 43. Waterloo Road saw the tram service to Stafford Road and Bushbury, but it was never used by trolleybuses except when enthusiasts ran special tours. Even then it was doubtful if the wires, dating from 1941, were energised and tours had to run downhill, literally in the case of the traffic inspector assigned to look after Sunbeam W 439 and the Nottingham Trolleybus Group in March 1962.

←——— 44. One of the last recorded closures of Molineux Street was on 24 May 1962, when HM the Queen visited the town to commemorate the 450th anniversary of the foundation of Wolverhampton Grammar School. The visit moved on to the town centre, where road closures forced the diversion of Fordhouses services along Lower Stafford Street wiring, installed in 1933. On that day, Sunbeam W 404 heads up Lower Stafford Street away from its usual route towards the town centre, where it will be manually turned round in Stafford Street by a team of transport department crews before heading for Bushbury Hill.

←——— 45. The Great Western Railway made Wolverhampton its northern headquarters after acquiring the Oxford, Worcester & Wolverhampton and Shrewsbury & Birmingham Railways. The imposing Stafford Road Works on both sides of the road also housed a Mechanics' Institute, while the buildings to the right included the sheds which stabled many King class locomotives used on the route to Birmingham Snow Hill, Banbury and London Paddington. This bridge, however, carried a mere link line from Oxley Sidings to Herbert Street Goods Depot. Its rebuilding from a Brunel-designed brick skew arch in 1937 allowed double-deckers on the route. Sunbeam W 449 heads for Wolverhampton in November 1963.

46. After leaving railway territory, Sunbeam W 455 loads passengers at Gorsebrook Road stop, on the bridge over the Birmingham Canal Navigations at the top of the flight of locks down to the Staffordshire & Worcestershire Canal known as the "Wolverhampton 21". This is also the nearest stop for the soon to be redundant Gas Works, and for Dunstall Park Racecourse. No racing on a Sunday, however, and this is the last day of service, 26 January 1963.

47.   Church Road was a regular turning point for Stafford Road trolleybuses until the 1960s. The stop took its name from the street opposite, rather than Oxley Moor Road where the loop is built. It also served Wingfoot Park, the Goodyear sports ground and for many years a popular venue for staff and public alike. Sunbeam F4 460 passes on the way to Fordhouses on 31 January 1962.

48. The Corporation was anxious to construct a dual carriageway and widen the narrow section of Stafford Road north of Oxley Moor Road. Work began towards the end of 1963, with the expectation that the trolleybuses would be removed before completion. Delays to motorbus deliveries put paid to that idea, so the overhead crews had to widen the wires with the road. Just two weeks before closure, the first section was commissioned and Sunbeam W 430 uses it under the last section of new trolleybus wiring, on its way to Fordhouses on 18 January 1963.

49. The Vine public house had not assumed this half-timbered form when trolleybuses first served the Stafford Road to Fordhouses on 9 March 1925. In the last days of the route in December 1963, Sunbeam W 447 has unloaded its passengers while Sunbeam W 441 has turned on the roundabout and awaits its departure time. The centre traction poles along the dual carriageway from the Three Tuns island at Wobaston Road were the only examples on the system.

CANNOCK ROAD:
BUSHBURY HILL, LOW HILL, AMOS LANE

50. The Cannock Road services for Bushbury Hill, Low Hill and Amos Lane all passed along Stafford Street, alongside the Wolverhampton & South Staffordshire College of Technology. Bushbury Hill services passed the others after turning from Wulfruna Street to the right, while Sunbeam W 442 waits at the 13 stand for Low Hill (Pear Tree), Sunbeam W 452 is at the 9 stand for Amos Lane and Sunbeam W 454 has its back to us at the 12/13 stand by the TA Drill hall for Merry Hill or Finchfield. November 24 1962

⟶ 51. Route 88 lasted barely two months with trolleybuses, and turned around the loop in Princes Square after its cross-town link to Jeffcock Road was cut in September 1963. Sunbeam F4 464 turns on the first day of the "new" Amos Lane service, 30 September 1963.

⟶ 52. Post-war Wolverhampton trolleybuses never carried traction batteries, so had to resort to primitive methods on the day of the Queen's visit, May 24 1962. For several hours crews and inspectors performed this operation in Stafford Street, here turning Sunbeam F4 470 to run to Bushbury Hill on route 3, while other Cannock Road services wait their turn further along Stafford Street.

53.   Sunbeam Ws 455 and 446, bunching
well on the cross-town route 3 in November 1963
to turn from Cannock Road to Stafford Street at
the spectacular Elephant and Castle public house.
The diversion wiring along Lower Stafford Street
for Fordhouses enters from the left.

———→ 54. The railway bridge carried the
Grand Junction Railway, the first main line
from Liverpool to Birmingham in 1837, across
Cannock Road in Park Village. Sunbeam W 452
heads for town from Low Hill on its cross-town
route 13 trip to Merry Hill in October 1963.

———→ 55.   The two-way junction from Park Lane to Cannock Road was only used by
service trolleybuses in one direction and Sunbeam W 443 will turn in front of the photographer on
its route 3 journey from Bushbury Hill to Fordhouses on 25 January 1964, the last Saturday of the
route.

56. The great inter-war housing estates expanded Wolverhampton to the north east and created a demand for bus services at first provided by motor buses. Trolleybuses came to the Cannock Road routes first to serve Bushbury Hill, on 30 January 1931. Sunbeam W 443 stands at the junction of Old Fallings Lane and Leacroft Avenue, on January 26 1964, the last day of operation. The trees in the background formed a striking landmark in the northern part of the town.

57. Low Hill and Amos Lane routes divided at the junction of Victoria Road, Thorneycroft Road and Bushbury Road. Towards the end of trolleybus operation, Sunbeam W 417 is heading from Low Hill across town to Finchfield, while Sunbeam W 403 is inbound from Amos Lane on the short-lived 88 rump of the cross-town route to Jeffcock Road in October 1963.

58. Cannock Road services branched at Park Lane in Park Village for Amos Lane and Low Hill (Pear Tree), and services began on 21 March 1932. The Amos Lane route originally terminated at the eponymous road, and trolleybuses had to use a triangular reverser. Sunbeam W 446 is seen at the site, about to cross Amos Lane. The route was the last to be extended, along Prestwood Road behind the vehicle, in 1956. Until September 1963 the route was numbered 9, but given the number 88 when its cross-town link with Jeffcock Road was severed.

59.   The Pheasant Inn extension of the Amos Lane trolleybus route opened on 24 June 1956, running along Prestwood Road West beyond Wolverhampton-bound Sunbeam W 446 to a large roundabout turning circle. This was near the end of trolleybuses on the route in early November 1963.

→ 60. The borough boundary with the Urban District of Wednesfield runs along the pavement at Blackhalve Lane, as Sunbeam W 405 heads up Cannock Road from Low Hill for town and Finchfield on route 12, on 23 October 1963. In the background, we observe the beginnings of Cannock Chase.

→ 61. Low Hill terminus was alongside the Pear Tree Inn, to the left of Sunbeam W 438, about to leave for the cross-town route 12 journey to Finchfield, while 447 has arrived from Merry Hill on a route 13 working in November 1963.

WEDNESFIELD

62. The first Wolverhampton trolleybuses were half a dozen Tilling Stevens TS6 with Dodson bodywork, replacing trams on the route to Wednesfield from 29 October 1923. The corporation had converted the trams to overhead wires only two years before and doubling the aerial display after years of surface-contact traction must have seemed almost risqué. This photograph of number 2, credited to Osmond Wildsmith, dates from 1925 and is usually cropped to remove the fleeting trolleybus turning on the second route to Fordhouses, opened on 9 January 1925. In 1933 the two routes, both operated by single-deckers, were linked to operate across town.

63.   From 1937, Wednesfield trolleybuses used Thornley Street, behind the TA Drill Hall, as their in-town terminus, branching off Broad Street just before Princes Square. Sunbeam W 402 waits its next trip on the 39th anniversary of the route, 29 October 1962.

64.   This bridge under the railway line from Wolverhampton to Stafford was the reason the route originally operated only single-deckers. The road was carved away for double deckers in early 1944. From Wednesfield they had to negotiate over the Great Western Railway, then under the LMS, then over the BCN canal bridge on which the photographer is standing. Sunbeam F4 467 heads for town on 29 October 1962.

65.　　The chimney sweep is a reminder that
there was no smokeless zone until the early
1970s. Sunbeam W 442 heads outbound along
Wednesfield Road in Heath Town, passing
Inkerman Street, on 29 October 1962.

⟶ 66. The first trolleybuses turned in
front of the "half-timbered" Dog & Partridge
public house until the route was extended to
Wood End in 1934. Sunbeam W 456 passes on
the route's 39th anniversary, 29 October 1962.

⟶ 67. By the 1960s, the Wood End Road turning circle was used only for rare workings
on route 6, but also proved useful for turning failures. Sunbeam W 448 uses the loop after cutting
short its route 59 journey to the Albion in August 1962.

68.   The penultimate route extension from Wood End to The Albion public house was opened on 10 January 1955. The mile-long extension had no reinforcing power supply, so if too many trolleybuses were under the wires the lights faded and speed dropped. Sunbeam W 447 stands at the terminus on 29 October 1962.

WILLENHALL AND WALSALL

69.   Until 1951 the Wolverhampton terminus for the joint route to Walsall was in Horseley Fields near Old Mill Street, where in April 1965 Sunbeam W 444 is passing on its way from the depot to gain St James Square terminus.

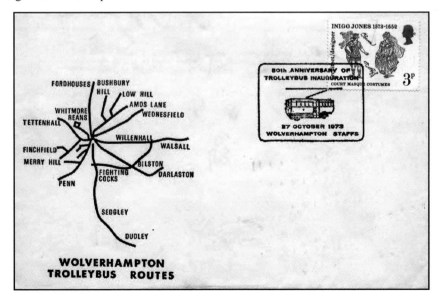

70.   The joint 29 Walsall route in action at St James Square in September 1965, with Walsall Sunbeam F4 351 (ex Ipswich 119), and Wolverhampton Sunbeam Ws 449 and 431 operating the 5 short working to Willenhall. 351's driver has so far failed to turn the blind, showing how the long word of Wolverhampton was squeezed onto the square Ipswich indicator box.

⟶ 71. Not only the trolleybuses were for it in the 1960s, churches were under threat too. Sunbeam W 431 working back to Wolverhampton on route 29 passes St Matthew's being demolished in Lower Horseley Fields at Lower Walsall Street in April 1964.

⟶ 72. At Portobello, trolleybuses crossed over the Grand Junction Railway, the first trunk line from the north to the Midlands. Guy BT 651 is on its way to Wolverhampton in April 1963.

73.　　The sun glints off Sunbeam F4 630 as it negotiates the wiring in Willenhall from Walsall Street to New Road at the Dale Cinema in August 1964. This was the terminus for short workings from Wolverhampton (route 5) and Walsall (unnumbered but nominally 29). It was also the turning loop for trolleybuses on route 25 to Bilston and Fighting Cocks in Bilston Street, behind 630.

74.   This is now Walsall territory, and Sunbeam W 428 is on learner duty, while Sunbeam F4 625 is resting at Willenhall in the layby in front of St Giles Parish Church on route 29 from Walsall to Wolverhampton in April 1965.

75.   Willenhall was drop forgers country, exemplified by the works of Armstrong Stevens, spanner manufacturers, on one corner of the junction on Walsall Road at the stop known either as "Crescent Road", to the right or "Board Schools", the building on the right. An unidentified Sunbeam W passes in October 1965.

76.   Another unidentified Wolverhampton Sunbeam W on route 29 heads in October 1965 for the encroaching works for the M6 motorway at Bentley, on Wolverhampton Road West at Bentley Mill Lane. The works would eventually bring a premature end to the route.

77.   The Walsall terminus was originally at the top of Park Street at Townend Bank, in front of an entertainment venue that was first a theatre then an ABC cinema. It was moved in 1950 to Townend Street, behind the cinema, which made for a less complicated manoeuvre. Ray Wilson photographed Wolverhampton Sunbeam F4 630 when nearly new in the early 1950s.The Walsall terminus was originally at the top of Park Street on Townend Bank in front of the entertainment complex, first a theatre then an ABC cinema, but was moved in 1950 to Townend Street behind the cinema, which made for a less complicated manoeuvre. Ray Wilson photographed Wolverhampton Sunbeam F4 when nearly new in the early 1950s.

BILSTON AND DARLASTON

78.   Victoria Square was the first trolleybus terminus that enthusiasts visiting by train would see, with five routes terminating and the through service from Whitmore Reans to Bilston and Darlaston passing through. In addition, trolleybuses for Willenhall and Walsall would turn into Horseley Fields for their terminus at St James Square. In June 1963 Sunbeam F4 480 is using the terminal loop to take up a duty on the 47 short working to Bilston, while Sunbeam W 426 on route 2 to Darlaston is having some attention from the service crew with one of the two Robinson-bodied tower wagons bought in 1959.

79.   Sunbeam W 415 has just turned from Victoria Square into Pipers Row for Bilston and Darlaston in July 1965, leaving the Five Ways island where trolleybuses turn for Horseley Fields and the Willenhall and Walsall terminus.

◀━━━━━━━ 80. Not a single building in this photograph of Sunbeam F4 471 turning from Pipers Row to Bilston Street in November 1963 is still standing. The tracks of Midland Metro now run where the former Midland Red garage stands, while behind the photographer is the wishbone bridge over a large traffic island for the inner ring road.

◀━━━━━━━ 81. Sunbeam F4 457 on route 7 for Wolverhampton and Whitmore Reans in Bilston Street is passing the bus garage and the cattle market. Commercial Road power station, built to serve the town's trams and other electricity consumers, is in production in July 1965

82.   Electric trains now run over, and Midland Metro trams run under, bridge 84 (Butlers Ales). Back in July 1965 both were a distant dream as Sunbeam F4 473 passes under it and bridge 83A (M&B Export), which carried a siding to a canal basin in May 1964.

←——— 83. A pristine Sunbeam F4 478 on route 2 from Wolverhampton is about to cross Stow Heath Lane at the borough boundary, where Lorain Surface Contact System trams changed to overhead, on the last Saturday of the route, August 7 1965. After today, 478 would be the last 8ft wide Sunbeam in service, withdrawn on October 31 1965.

←——— 84. Bilston's Clinic was the main layover point in the town for trolleybuses like Sunbeam W 434 on the way in March 1965 to Wolverhampton and Whitmore Reans. Behind is the junction for the depot in Mount Pleasant and Willenhall on route 25.

85.   Sunbeam W 409 with its postwar body leaves Bilston Depot in Mount Pleasant for the last time to take up a route 47 working from Bilston to Wolverhampton. The trolleybus is turning from Mount Pleasant to Lichfield Street on the last day of operation, 8 August 1965.

← ———— 86. The boys in their drainpipe trousers and winklepicker shoes are hurrying to catch Sunbeam W 422 on its trip to Moxley and Darlaston, while Sunbeam W 446, pulling out of Fraser Street reverser, shows Bilston on its blind despite the route number 2. It has come from Mount Pleasant depot this last Sunday, August 8 1965, of trolleybuses on the busy route and is to set off for Wolverhampton and Whitmore Reans. That night, 446 would be the last Darlaston trolleybus, 422 the last on route 2 to Whitmore Reans.

← ———— 87. The turning loop on Great Bridge Road was added to the system in 1949, partly to remove regular turnbacks at the Fryer Street reverser in Bilston, partly to serve better the factories in the area. Sunbeam F4 621 is on a route 7 cross-town trip to Whitmore Reans and is about to pick up at the stop outside the Quasi Arc welding supplies factory in November 1963.

88. Sunbeam F4 477 is about to run the short distance back to Moxley Road on a 47 route working from Great Bridge Road (the destination blind would read "Bilston") in November 1963. A Midland "Red" bus is on a trip towards Tipton. Across the fields modern travellers can alight at the Bradley Lane stop of Midland Metro.

89.   This island at Moxley is where the trolleybuses from Darlaston joined the A41 Holyhead Road. In November 1964 Sunbeam W 431 was on its way to Whitmore Reans.

90.   Quite why the driver of Sunbeam W 446 decided to display a "0" in the box which should show either black or, at worst, the end of the blind with some white showing is a mystery. In November 1964, the trolleybus is setting out from Pinfold Street, Darlaston on its 41 minute journey through Bilston and Wolverhampton to Whitmore Reans, having turned round the island behind the coal lorry.

WILLENHALL, BILSTON
AND FIGHTING COCKS

91.   Sunbeam W 433 stands at Willenhall Bilston Street terminus of the belt route 25 in late
September 1962, when school is obviously out.

← 92. The crane on the left and the 25kV electrification gantry on the right are precursors of change on the railways as well as the road. It was work needed to raise this bridge just yards from its Willenhall terminus to accommodate the wires that forced conversion of the trolleybus route in late October 1964. Guy BT 652 crosses the bridge in July of that year, just after starting the 22-minute trip to Bilston and Fighting Cocks.

← 93. The route served a mixture of suburban housing and industry, typified near the Willenhall end by this scene at the Cock Inn by Silvester Road, where Willenhall Road becomes Bilston Road. Sunbeam W 410 travels from Bilson to Willenhall, in July 1964.

94. The 25 route replaced two company-operated tram services and so was almost completely outside the County Borough of Wolverhampton. Bilston depot was a former company shed, operated by the BET subsidiary, Wolverhampton District Electric Tramways, until acquired by the Corporation on 1 September 1928, six days after it ceased to operate tram services within the borough. Little has changed as Sunbeam W 426 emerges onto Mount Pleasant from the narrow entrance to turn to the photographer's left and take up service on the 25 route to Bilston and Fighting Cocks, in July 1964.

95.   Bilston Town Hall marked the halfway point of route 25, and Sunbeam W 417 has come out of Mount Pleasant at the end of the white buildings, down Lichfield Street and has tripped the frog to turn right into Church Street. In July 1964 it is being followed by two trolleybuses on the Darlaston "main line", Sunbeam W 418 on route 2 for Darlaston, and Sunbeam W 425 on a 47 short working to Great Bridge Road, Bilston.

96.   On the same day, Sunbeam W 410 crosses the Western Region main line from Birkenhead to Birmingham and Paddington in Church Street, on the way to Fighting Cocks. The two shops it is passing hung over the railway and have now been demolished to form an access point for the new Bilston Central stop of Midland Metro.

97.   John Thompson's works was a major employer and supplier of boilers for power stations, as well as engineering goods and chassis for local motor manufacturers. Its premises occupied both sides of Millfields Road. When a large boiler was sent out, the local roads were closed so it could pass. Sunbeam W 411 has travelled under the Stour Valley West Coast Main Line and crossed Ettingshall Road, on its way from Fighting Cocks to Bilston and Willenhall, in August 1964.

98.   Industrial terraced housing was typical of this older section of Bilston on the outskirts of Wolverhampton. Sunbeam W 449 is travelling from Fighting Cocks along Parkfield Road at Myrtle Street feeder, near Rooker Avenue in September 1964.

99. The company trams turned from Parkfield Road towards Dudley at Fighting Cocks and there remained a vestige of this practice up to the end, with one working towards Sedgley every morning. However, this is Sunbeam W 408 on tour, using the connection on 5 April 1964.

100. Until 1949, route 25 trolleybuses used the connection in both directions to reach the Dudding Road terminus of "main line" Fighting Cocks trolleybuses from Wolverhampton. In May 1949 the practice ceased with the construction of a new junction and wiring along Goldthorn Hill Road. Sunbeam F4 475 crosses from Parkfield Road in the final stages of its trip from Willenhall. It is passing the Fighting Cocks Inn on the right, as it heads for the terminus at Ward Road in December 1963.

101. Sunbeam W 417 has left the Ward Road layover point in the quiet suburban Fighting Cocks terminal of route 25 and is heading along Goldthorn Hill Road towards Bilston and Willenhall in June 1964. Just visible on the skyline are the blast furnaces of Bilston Steelworks, owned in private days by Stewarts & Lloyds.

FIGHTING COCKS,
SEDGLEY AND DUDLEY

102.   The Friday evening rush hour for Dudley route trolleybuses on 28 August 1964. Sunbeam W 416 is leaving Bilston Street on a short working 61 to Sedgley; behind, Sunbeam W 453 will go through to Dudley on the 58 and at the back, Sunbeam F4 626 is on another 61 working to Sedgley. The Sedgley workings could end either at the Bull Ring or the Green Dragon. The unconnected wiring runs along the rest of Bilston Street to Pipers Row.

103.   On Sunday 22 May 1966, the National Trolleybus Association organised a tour using its preserved Huddersfield Karrier MS2 541, the first on any system by a "foreign" privately-owned trolleybus, so the upper destination indicator had to show locals where it came from. The NTA susbstituted its lower blind with a Wolverhampton example, though there was no "4" on a Huddersfield trolleybus number blind. The Karrier chassis was built by Sunbeam in Wolverhampton in 1946. Native Sunbeam W 424 passes 541 to reach its loading point in Bilston Street on route 58 for Dudley. On the last day, 5 March 1967, the NTA had two preserved trolleybuses on tour, Rotherham 44 and Wolverhampton 654.

104. The building on the right, behind the Wolverhampton Corporation Seddon road sweeper, is the Fighting Cocks Inn, from which the district and the trolleybus termini take their name. Sunbeam F4 468 has crossed the junction with Goldthorn Hill and Parkfield Roads and back into Wolverhampton, on the last stages of its 58 route journey from Dudley in July 1964.

———————➤ 105. The terminal and passing wiring at Dudding Road date from 1934, replacing an inconvenient turning circle at the road junction in the previous picture used by 8 and 25 route trolleybuses to Fighting Cocks. The road sign says firmly "Trolley Buses Only" and is preserved at the Black Country Living Museum in Dudley. Sunbeam W 408 stands at the layover point on a shortworking 8 from Wolverhampton, while Sunbeam W 439 passes on a 58 working from Dudley in April 1964.

———————➤ 106. Sunbeam W 408 sets out in June 1964 on its trip on route 58 to Dudley up Wolverhampton Road from Fighting Cocks on the long climb to Sedgley Beacon, one of the highest points of the Black Country. With the Black Country laid out in the distance, the chimney and cooling tower of Wolverhampton's Commercial Road power station show where the power for the trolleybus is generated.

107.   Nearing the top of the hill on Wolverhampton Road at Springfield Road, under Sedgley Beacon, Sunbeam W 443 on a 58 to Dudley in May 1964 passes traction poles that show their origin as supports for the Wolverhampton District Electric Tramways Company's overhead wires, complete with BET "Wheel and Magnet" pole base.

——→ 108. The streets of Sedgley are quiet this weekday lunchtime in May 1964 and Sunbeam F4 466 pulls away from the Bull Ring up Dudley Street on the way to Dudley on route 58. The driver has failed to set the "5" correctly, however, and the service number showing reminds us that until 1948, this was the 8B. There is a full turning circle in front of the Clifton cinema for short workings on route 61 in either direction.

——→ 109. The conductor of Sunbeam W 426 prepares to take up passengers waiting outside the Green Dragon public house on a 58 route trip from Dudley in February 1967. This is the turning loop for route 61 workings from Wolverhampton to Sedgley and the trolleybus is passing from Burton Road to Kent Street at Jew's Lane.

WOLVERHAMPTON CORP TWYS & MTRS
SINGLE DECK TROLLEYBUS

Body: Dodson B40C 1923.	
Chassis: Tilling Stevens TS6	Scale: 4 mm = 1Foot.
Fleet No. 1 – 6.	
DRAWING No. TB60	

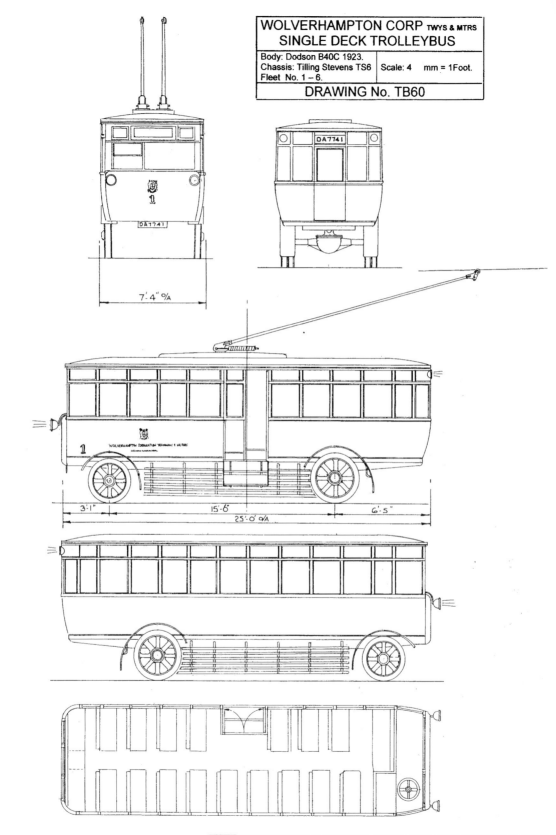

7'-4" O/A

DA7741

3'-1"   15'-6"   6'-5"

25'-0" O/A

SCALE
FEET   0   1   2   3   4   5   6   7   8   9   10   11   12

DRAWN BY :- TERRY RUSSELL, "CHACESIDE", ST. LEONARDS PARK, HORSHAM, W.SUSSEX. RH13 6E
SEND 4 FIRST CLASS STAMPS FOR COMPLETE LIST OF PUBLIC TRANSPORT DRAWING

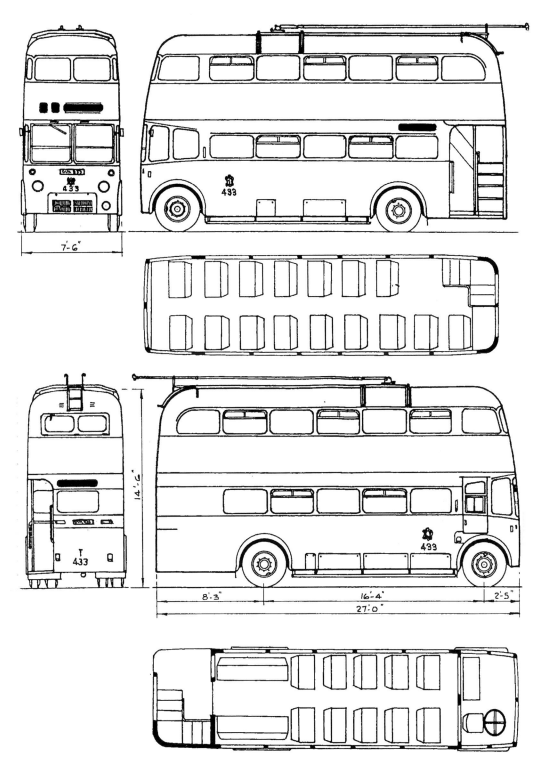

7'-6"

14'-6"

8'-3"   16'-4"   2'-5"

27'-0"

SCALE
FEET   0   1   2   3   4   5   6   7   8   9   10   11   12

WOLVERHAMPTON CORP TRANSPORT
D/DECK 2 AXLE TROLLEYBUS

| BUILT: 1946. CHASSIS: SUNBEAM W | SCALE: 4 MM = 1 FOOT |
| REBODIED ROE 1959. FLEET No.T433 | |

DRAWING No. TB31

110. This was the point where Wolverhampton trolleybuses passed from Staffordshire into Worcestershire, as Dudley was an enclave of Worcestershire until West Midlands County Council was created in the 1970s. Sunbeam W 427 is on Burton Road and has passed the junction with The Broadway on a 58 route working to Sedgley and Wolverhampton in February 1967.

111. The final run into Dudley was along the terraced Wolverhampton Street from Eve Hill. Sunbeam Ws 454 and 444 are bunching nicely at Charlton Street, as they near the end of their route 58 trip in August 1964.

112. The Dudley turning circle at Stone Street was only half the size when services began in 1927. It was extended to go round the former market in 1943, and the long shelter where Sunbeam F4 613 is standing in December 1962 is evidence of the popularity of the destination for day trippers to Dudley. The main attraction was Dudley Zoo and Castle, entered through arches designed by London Zoo architect Berthold Lubetkin's firm Tecton in the late 1930s and featuring some of his iconic animal enclosures and other structures.

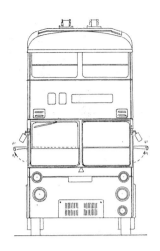

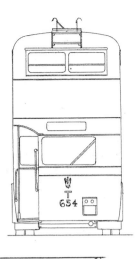

FLEET DETAILS

No. 456 – 481 Sunbeam F4   built 1948.
No. 482 – 499 Guy BT   built 1948.
No. 600 – 607 Guy BT   built 1949.
No. 608 – 630 Sunbeam F4 built 1949/50.
No. 631 – 654 Guy BT   built 1949/50.

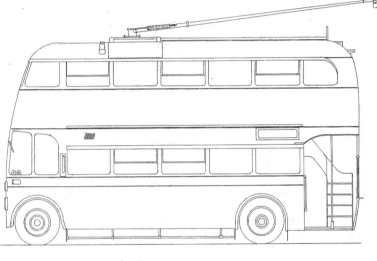

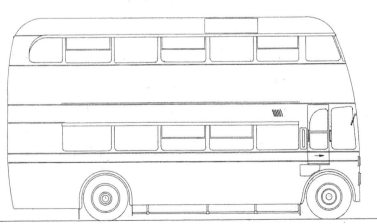

WOLVERHAMPTON CORPORATION
AXLE DOUBLE DECK TROLLEYBUS

: Park Royal 1948/1950
sis: Guy BT or Sunbeam F4
No. 456 - 499 & 600 – 654.

Scale: 4   mm = 1 Foot.

DRAWING No. TB59

SCALE
FEET   0   1   2   3   4   5   6   7   8   9   10   11   12

DRAWN BY:-TERRY RUSSELL, "CHACESIDE", ST. LEONARDS PARK, HORSHAM, W.SUSSEX. RH13 6EG.
SEND 4 FIRST CLASS STAMPS FOR COMPLETE LIST OF PUBLIC TRANSPORT DRAWINGS.

DEPOTS

113.   Cleveland Road was home to most of Wolverhampton's trolleybus fleet and dates from the first electric trams of 1902. The road was fortunately a quiet backwater and manoeuvres like these could be carried out in relative safety. The crew of Sunbeam F4 600 have evidently taken the wrong road to bring the vehicle home. Transferring the poles is easier than backing up. Guy BT 496, backing out of the shed, is probably going to provide the substitute vehicle on the busy Dudley route in April 1963.

114.   No 11 (DA 9011) Tilling Stevens/Dodson photographed by Ray Wilson outside Cleveland Road Depot in 1932. The depot remained unaltered throughout the trolleybus period. It was demolished in 1977 and rebuilt to incorporate the later, lower level, Bilston Street motorbus garage. It is now a large covered car park.

115.   Turning a trolleybus like Sunbeam W 426 was an everyday event at the ex-WDET tramway depot at Bilston. There was also a turntable at Sedgley depot (1927-31) and it and the Bilston example briefly existed together. Bilston housed trolleybuses from 1930, with the conversion of the Willenhall-Bilston-Fighting Cocks route. It also provided vehicles for the trunk Darlaston-Bilston-Wolverhampton-Whitmore Reans routes. It was effectively an outstation of Cleveland Road and had no permanent allocation. The dog belonged to Inspector Howard Davies, who lived in the former WDET manager's house at the depot entrance.

116.   Park Lane, opened in 1937 and briefly a trolleybus-only depot, was on route 3 to Bushbury Hill, opposite the Guy Motors factory where many trolleybuses were built, near the Meadows engine factory that provided diesel engines for buses. In later years many of the rebodied Sunbeam Ws were allocated there to serve the Cannock Road and Wednesfield routes. 455, numerically the last of these vehicles, passes on the way to Bushbury Hill in December 1963, while an unidentified sister stands on the circuit erected around the depot to provide a test track.

AFTERMATH

117.   "We'll give them away," said Alderman Frank Mansell, chairman of Wolverhampton Transport Committee, and enthusiasts took him at his word. Sunbeam F4 616, dating from 1948 with a Park Royal 8ft wide body and unusual double reduction rear axle, found a home at the Railway Preservation Society's premises at Hednesford in Staffordshire. Seen there on 12 September 1965, two years after withdrawal, the vehicle has been moved several times since, but has never travelled under its own power. It is currently at the Birmingham and Midland Motor Omnibus Trust at Wythall.

←——— 118. Park Royal-bodied Guy BT 654 was the last ever Guy trolleybus in 1950 and was preserved by the fledgling National Trolleybus Association after its withdrawal on 8 August 1965. By 1967 it had been repainted back to 1950s style, though retaining the 1960s direction flashers, and was used for a tour of the Dudley route on the last day. On that day, outside Cleveland Road Depot, it is being backed to the extent of the cut-off wires towards Bilston Road. The vehicle is not likely to have carried route 8B in service, as the route numbers were changed (in this case to 58) before it was delivered. 654 is also in store.

←——— 119. The Black Country Museum Transport group has rescued 1931 Guy BTX 78 from a field in Ireland. It requires a lot of work to restore it and its Guy bodywork to running order, but at least it is now under cover in the Museum depot awaiting suitable funding. Ray Wilson photographed sister vehicle 73 travelling through Queen Square in the 1930s.

120.   The preservation success story is 433, the last utility trolleybus delivered by Sunbeam in 1946. It received a new Roe body in 1959 and was stored under cover in various places until safely delivered to the Black Country Living Museum in the 1970s. A number of similar vehicles were earmarked for preservation, and many of their parts are incorporated into 433. It is in regular service at weekends at the museum in Tipton Road, Dudley, on a circuit made largely from equipment rescued from Wolverhampton and Walsall and is seen alongside the clock which used to stand in Victoria Square.

MP Middleton Press

EVOLVING THE ULTIMATE RAIL ENCYCLOPEDIA

Easebourne Lane, Midhurst, West Sussex.
GU29 9AZ Tel:01730 813169

www.middletonpress.co.uk email:info@middletonpress.co.uk

A-0 906520 B-1 873793 C-1 901706 D-1 904474

OOP Out of Print at time of printing - Please check current availability **BROCHURE AVAILABLE SHOWING NEW TITLES**